The Missions of California

Mission
San Miguel Arcángel

Kathleen J. Edgar and Nancy A. Edgar

The Rosen Publishing Group's
PowerKids Press™
New York

Published in 2000 by The Rosen Publishing Group, Inc.
29 East 21st Street, New York, NY 10010

Photo Credits and Photo Illustrations: pp. 1,17, 18, 21, 27, 35, 36, 42, 43, 44, 45, 48, 50, 51, 52, 57 by Cristina Taccone; pp. 4, 20, 26, 32, 39 © Shirley Jordan; p. 6 © The Bridgeman Art Library International Ltd.; pp. 8, 12 © Seaver Center for Western History Research, LA County Museum of Natural History; p. 9 © AP/Wide World; pp. 11, 14, 25, 41 by Tim Hall; pp. 15, 34 © CORBIS/Bettman; pp. 16, 33, 36, 37, 40 © Michael K. Ward; p. 19 © Eda Rogers; p. 22, 49 © SuperStock; pp. 24, 31, 38 © Santa Barbara Mission Archive—Library; p. 46 © The Huntington Library, Art Collections, and Botanical Gardens, San Marino, California/SuperStock; p. 47 © Stock Montage.

First Edition

Book Design: Danielle Primiceri

Book Layout: Felicity Erwin

Editorial Consultant Coordinator: Karen Fontanetta, M.A., Curator, Mission San Miguel Arcángel
Editorial Consultant: Karen Fontanetta, M.A.
Historical Photo Consultants: Thomas L. Davis, M.Div., M.A. and Michael K. Ward, M.A.

Edgar, Kathleen J.
    Mission San Miguel Arcángel / by Kathleen J. Edgar and Nancy A. Edgar
       p. cm. — (The missions of California)
    Includes bibliographical references and index.
    Summary: Discusses Mission San Miguel Arcángel from its founding in 1797 to the present day, including the reasons for Spanish colonization in California and the effects of colonization on the California Indians.
    ISBN 0-8239-5502-8 (lib. bdg.)
    1. Mission San Miguel Arcángel (San Miguel, Calif.)—History Juvenile literature.
2. Spanish mission buildings—California—San Miguel Region—History Juvenile literature.
3. Franciscans—California—San Miguel Region—History Juvenile literature. 4. Indians of North America—Missions—California—San Miguel Region—History Juvenile literature. 5. California—History—To 1846 Juvenile literature. [1. Mission San Miguel Arcángel (San Miguel, Calif.)—History.
2. Missions—California. 3. Indians of North America—Missions—California. 4. California—History—To 1846.] I. Edgar, Nancy A. II. Title. III. Series.
F869. M666E34 1999
979.4'78—dc21
                                                99-20507
                                                CIP

Manufactured in the United States of America

Contents

Spanish Explorers Come to California

Mission San Miguel Arcángel

On the outskirts of the sleepy little town of San Miguel, the past is preserved at Mission San Miguel Arcángel. As cars race down the highway in the distance, the quiet mission stands as a reminder of Spanish efforts to colonize the land that is today the state of California. At one end of the mission stands the church, an off-white building with a red tile roof. Next to the church is a short wall with several entrances. One entrance is a large arch, which transports visitors who step through it back in time.

Mission San Miguel Arcángel was founded by Spanish friars and soldiers in 1797 and built by the Salinan Indians. The friars, called *frays* in Spanish, were religious men who devoted their lives to the Catholic religion. They were sent by the Spanish government to colonize lands in the Americas. The friars established a chain of missions along the coast, hoping to convert California Indians to Catholicism and teach them the Spanish way of life. Mission San Miguel Arcángel was the 16th of 21 missions founded in California between 1769 and 1823.

Spain Explores the Americas

Spain's interest in California began in 1493, after explorer Christopher Columbus brought back news of the lands he called the New World. Although American Indians had lived on these lands for thousands of years, the Americas were unknown to European settlers until this time. The Spanish and other Europeans were eager to explore these lands and claim them for themselves.

◀ *The church of Mission San Miguel Arcángel.*

The Spanish were interested in the New World for a number of reasons. They wanted to make their empire larger and become a more powerful nation. They hoped to find gold, spices, and other riches. They also wanted to spread the teachings of the Christian religion.

New Spain

The king of Spain wanted to claim land in the Americas, but Spain didn't have many citizens who wanted to settle there. In order to take command of these lands without sending a large number of Spanish settlers, the Spanish government decided instead to turn the American

This picture, painted around 1550, shows Cortés entering the Aztec lands.

Indians into Spanish citizens. They would do this by teaching them the Spanish language, customs, and religion. In 1519, a Spanish soldier and explorer named Hernán Cortés went to the area that today is Mexico and conquered the great Aztec empire. The Spanish claimed this land and called it New Spain. They established a capital that they called Mexico City and set up a government under a leader called a viceroy. The king sent Spanish soldiers and friars to build religious settlements, or missions, that would teach the conquered people in New Spain about the Spanish religion and way of life.

Alta California

After the Spanish claimed New Spain, they became interested in some of the land to the north. This was what is now California and the part of Mexico that is called the Baja Peninsula. The state of California was then called Alta (upper) California, while the Baja Peninsula was known as Baja (lower) California.

The Spanish explorer Juan Rodríguez Cabrillo sailed to Alta California in 1542, where he found what was later called San Diego Bay. Cabrillo and his men claimed the land for Spain by planting a cross in the ground to represent their country and its religion.

In 1602, another Spanish explorer, Sebastían Vizcaíno, traveled to Alta California. He sailed around what is now the Bay of Monterey. Since neither Cabrillo nor

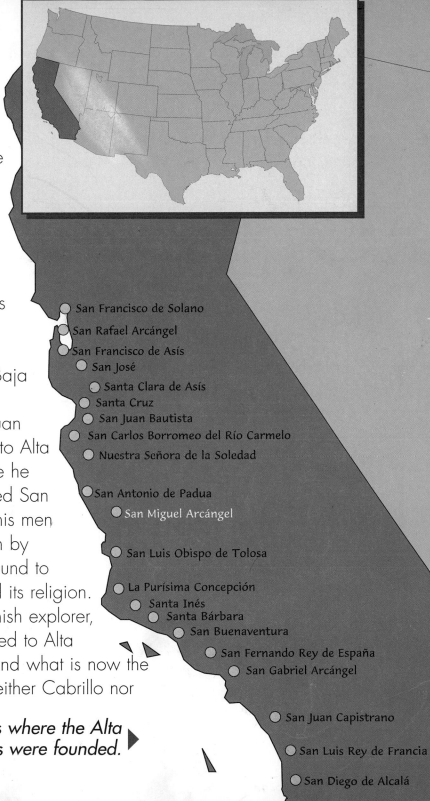

This map shows where the Alta California missions were founded. ▶

San Francisco de Solano
San Rafael Arcángel
San Francisco de Asís
San José
Santa Clara de Asís
Santa Cruz
San Juan Bautista
San Carlos Borromeo del Río Carmelo
Nuestra Señora de la Soledad
San Antonio de Padua
San Miguel Arcángel
San Luis Obispo de Tolosa
La Purísima Concepción
Santa Inés
Santa Bárbara
San Buenaventura
San Fernando Rey de España
San Gabriel Arcángel
San Juan Capistrano
San Luis Rey de Francia
San Diego de Alcalá

Vizcaíno found gold or rich nations to conquer, the Spanish did not think it was worth the time and money necessary to colonize Alta California.

It wasn't until 1769 that the Spanish sent men to begin the Alta California missions. At that time, Russian settlers were moving down toward Alta California from Alaska. The Spanish king, Carlos III, feared that colonists from Russia would take over these lands if he didn't act. King Carlos III ordered the government in New Spain to establish two missions in Alta California quickly—one in San Diego and another in Monterey, about 450 miles to the north.

▲
Captain Don Gaspár de Portolá.

The Spanish Settle Alta California

The government in New Spain sent five expeditions under the military command of Captain Don Gaspár de Portolá. A Franciscan friar named Fray Junípero Serra was chosen as the president of the mission system in Alta California and accompanied one of the groups. Serra had devoted his life to missionary work in New Spain, and he came to Alta California when he was 55 years old.

The expeditions included soldiers, friars, and Indians who had converted to Christianity at missions in New Spain. Three ships, the *San Carlos*, the *San Antonio*, and the *San José*, sailed up the coast. Two groups traveled over the desert land of New Spain. All five groups were to meet near San

Diego Bay at the beginning of July. The journey was difficult, and many men became sick. The *San José* and its crew were lost at sea. More than half of the 219 men who started the journey to Alta California died.

The Spanish ships carried many materials the friars would need to begin the missions, including food supplies and religious articles like crosses, statues, and robes. Other supplies were loaded on the backs of the pack mules that made the overland journey. Those who traveled over land herded cattle to Alta California from missions in New Spain.

The groups met in San Diego, and on July 16, 1769, Fray Serra founded Mission San Diego de Alcalá, the first mission in Alta California. It would be almost another 30 years before the Spanish would begin to build Mission San Miguel Arcángel.

When the first mission was founded in Alta California in 1769, many American Indians lived there in small villages. In contrast, the eastern coast of North America had many large cities, such as Boston, New York, and Philadelphia. Members of 13 eastern colonies signed the Declaration of Independence seven years later, in 1776.

The Salinan Indians

The Salinans

Before the Spanish colonized Alta California, about 300,000 California Indians lived there. They lived in many different tribes, and many of the tribes spoke different languages. The California Indians of the San Miguel area mainly belonged to the Salinan tribe, although some may have been Chumash Indians.

The Salinans lived like many other groups of California Indians. Although the Salinans did not have a written history, people who study past civilizations, called archaeologists, have learned about the Salinans by carefully digging up sites where villages used to be. They have uncovered artifacts, such as tools and weapons, that show how the Salinan Indians lived many years ago.

Hunting and Gathering

The lifestyle of the Salinans was based on the natural world. Their homes, diet, work, and religion were all linked to nature. The Salinans ate what food they could collect, hunt, or catch. Much of the Salinans' daily life was spent looking for plants, animals, fish, and insects. Salinan women did most of the gathering. They collected roots, seeds, berries, and nuts, including acorns. They also searched for insects and worms.

Acorns were an important source of nutrition for the Salinans, as they were for many California Indians. Acorns were used in soups, cakes, and breads. The Salinans collected acorns in the fall and stored them for later use. However, acorns are poisonous and can cause sickness and even death. To make the acorns safe to eat, the Salinan women

The Salinan Indians fished with spears or nets. ▶

▲

Salinan women wore skirts like this one.

prepared them in a special way. First they ground the acorns by crushing them between two rocks, called a mortar and pestle. They placed the acorn flour in a sandy pit or a basket and poured hot water over it. This had to be done 10 times to make the acorn flour safe to eat.

The Salinan men fished with nets woven from grass. They hunted with spears, and bows and arrows, for deer, ducks, rabbits, squirrels, and birds. Their arrowheads and spear tips were made of rocks, chipped to form a hard point that could pierce an animal's skin. The Salinan men used strong, flexible tree branches to make their bows. They made bow strings from vegetable stalks or animal tendons, called sinews.

Homes

The Salinans built their homes in the shape of a cone, using materials that grew in the area. They used wood to make a cone-shaped frame, then tied layers of brush and tule grass thatching to it. The thatch worked like shingles to keep the rain out.

The Salinans lived in villages of 30 to 300 people. They moved their villages at different times during the year. Since they lived off of the land, they had to move when water or food in the area became scarce. They also moved when their homes became old, weathered, or unstable. In the fall, the Salinans moved temporarily to shelters near forests of oak trees so they could harvest as many acorns as possible.

Dress

Throughout much of the year, the Salinan men wore little or no clothing. The women wore skirts made out of bark, grass, or animal hides. In cooler weather, men and women draped hides over their shoulders for warmth. The Salinans wore necklaces made of abalone shells. Both men and women wore their hair long.

Religion

The Salinans believed many spirits were at work in nature. They believed that medicine men, or shamans, were able to cure illnesses by chasing away evil spirits. The shamans treated the sick by dancing, singing, and using herbal medicines.

The Salinans honored the spirits with ceremonies. They also performed rituals to acknowledge deaths, weddings, hunting trips, births, and when boys and girls entered into adulthood. These ceremonies included singing and dancing. Sometimes the Salinans painted their bodies or wore special costumes for the occasion.

The Salinans had a lot of personal freedom. They set their own work schedule and found time to enjoy games, singing, and dancing. They were free to travel on hunting trips, to trade with other tribes, and to visit other villages. When the Spanish came to Alta California, the Salinans' way of life changed forever.

The Mission System

Friars and Soldiers

Before the Spanish came to Alta California, they had already founded many missions in New Spain and Baja California. They knew that the best way to draw California Indians to the missions was to provide them with food and other gifts. After the Indians began to live at the missions, they could be taught the Spanish language, customs, and religion.

Although the Spanish government wanted to build missions to create more Spanish citizens and claim land for Spain, the friars went to the missions because they were eager to teach California Indians about the Catholic faith. They believed that only Catholics would go to heaven after they died, and they wanted to save the American Indians' souls.

Soldiers accompanied the friars on the journey to Alta California.

Soldiers were sent to help with the building of the mission complex, to watch over the Indians at the mission, and to protect the complex against local California Indians who didn't want the Spanish on their lands. All of the missions had four or five soldiers that lived in the complex. In some areas, the Spanish built forts called presidios to protect the missions from attack.

◀ *The friars thought that they were helping the California Indians by bringing them to the missions.*

15

The Spanish and the Salinans

The Salinans lived very differently than the Europeans did. Because of their differences, the Spanish regarded the Salinans as people who

were "uncivilized," or as children who needed to be taught to live "properly." These prejudices were based on many things, including the fact that the Salinans wore little or no clothing, while the Spanish men wore shirts, jackets, and trousers, and the Spanish women wore floor-length dresses. The Spanish saw the Salinan Indians as inferior because they were not educated in schools like many Europeans, they lived in

The friars taught the Indians about Christianity and the Spanish way of life.

temporary homes, and they worshipped many spirits instead of the Christian god. The Spanish wanted to help the Salinans by teaching them how to farm, speak the Spanish language, and follow the Christian religion. The Spanish thought that teaching the Indians how to live like Spaniards was in the best interest of the Indians. They didn't realize that the Salinans led productive lives on their own.

Children were easier to convert than adults because they grew up in the mission system.

When California Indians joined a mission and converted to Christianity, they were called neophytes, which meant that they were new to the faith. Neophytes had to live at the mission and were not allowed to leave without the friars' permission. The friars feared that if the neophytes left the mission, they might never return.

The Spanish hoped to train the neophytes in the Spanish way of life in 10 years. After this period of time, the Spanish planned to turn the mission lands over to the Indians. The Indians would operate the mission as Spanish citizens and pay taxes to the Spanish government. The land would remain under the control of New Spain. This process of taking control of the land away from religious leaders and giving it to the government is called secularization.

While the original plan may have been to take over California Indian lands only to return them later, this did not happen. European, Mexican, and United States settlers would keep most of the lands that once belonged to California Indian tribes.

The Founding of Mission San Miguel Arcángel

Fray Lasuén

Mission San Miguel Arcángel was founded 28 years after Fray Serra founded the first mission in Alta California. Fray Serra died in 1784, and Fray Fermin Francisco de Lasuén became the new mission president on February 6, 1785. As president of the missions in Alta California, Lasuén made sure that each mission had everything it needed. He was also in charge of founding new missions. Fray Lasuén founded Mission San Miguel Arcángel.

This sign commemorates the mission's founding.

Choosing a Site

In 1795, the governor of California, Governor Diego Borica, felt that there was too large a gap between Mission San Luis Obispo de Tolosa and Mission San Antonio de Padua. It was more than a day's journey, and the Spanish did not like to travel at night through Indian lands. Governor Borica sent an expedition to find a suitable site for a new mission between the two that were already there. Fray Buenaventura Sitjar of Mission San Antonio de Padua and a few soldiers formed this expedition. Fray Sitjar wrote to Fray Lasuén that he had found a good spot with the necessary supplies of water and timber nearby.

Governor Borica wrote to the viceroy of New Spain, Viceroy Branciforte, to ask for permission to build the mission and for $1,000

A statue of Fray Lasuén. ▶

The Salinas river, outside of the mission.

for supplies. On August 19, 1796, Viceroy Branciforte wrote to say that the building could begin.

The site that Fray Sitjar chose for Mission San Miguel Arcángel was near the Salinas River. Located in a fertile valley with rich soil, the land was ideal for farming and ranching. The site was also near a large Salinan village called Sagshpileel. The Spanish hoped that many Salinans from this village would join the mission.

On July 25, 1797, Fray Lasuén founded Mission San Miguel Arcángel. Accompanied by Fray Sitjar and soldiers, Fray Lasuén blessed the spot, raised a cross, and performed a Catholic church service called a Mass. Fray Sitjar and a friar named Fray Antonio de la Concepción Horra were the first missionaries at Mission San Miguel Arcángel.

Salinans Come to the Mission

Many of the Salinans who came to the founding had friends and relatives who lived at Mission San Antonio de Padua and at Mission San Luis Obispo. They were interested in learning more about the Spanish way of life, but mostly, they were attracted by the steady supply of food that the mission could provide.

After the founding ceremony, the friars baptized 15 Salinan children. Baptism is a ritual that is held when someone is accepted into the Christian religion. The friars were pleased that the Salinans wanted to join Mission San Miguel Arcángel.

The Spanish needed the Salinans' help to build the mission complex. Some of the Salinans wanted to try the Spanish tools. The Spanish used axes made of metal, which could chop down trees quickly. The Indians used stone and wood tools, which didn't cut wood as easily. Other Salinans were attracted to the mission by gifts of food, beads, and fabrics offered by the Spanish in return for their work. Building began right away.

Mission San Miguel Arcángel is named after Saint Michael the Archangel. In paintings and statues, Saint Michael is often shown with his sword raised, ready to slay a dragon. He is said to guard people from the devil.

21

Building Mission San Miguel Arcángel

Temporary Shelters and Early Buildings

After the founding ceremony, Fray Lasuén left the mission. Fray Sitjar was in charge, and Fray Horra assisted him. The friars, soldiers, and the Salinans at the mission built temporary shelters out of wooden planks and thatch, designed to last only until more permanent structures could be built.

After the shelters were built, the friars, soldiers, and neophytes began to make adobe bricks for more permanent buildings. The Spanish showed the Salinans how to mix mud, water, and straw to make adobe. The workers mixed the adobe with their feet and packed it into rectangular wooden molds. Once the bricks were molded, the workers placed them in the sun to dry. Mud was used to cement the bricks together to make walls. After the walls were completed, a roof was built of sticks and mud.

Fray Horra

Fray Sitjar, Fray Horra, and the neophytes at Mission San Miguel Arcángel worked hard. They had few supplies and there was much to be done. Fray Horra had trouble adjusting to mission life. Soon after he arrived at Mission San Miguel Arcángel, Fray Horra wrote to the viceroy in New Spain that the Franciscans in California were mistreating the neophytes. He said that the friars beat and shackled the Indians at the missions. Fray Horra did not like how the neophytes were treated, and he did not like being at Mission San Miguel Arcángel. The work was difficult, and he was far from his home, family, and culture. The stress of life at the mission was too much for Fray Horra. Before a

◀ *The neophytes worked hard to make enough adobe bricks to build the mission.*

23

month passed by, Horra became mentally unstable. He ranted, shouted, and shot at some of the Salinans. The Spanish sent him back to New Spain.

Two New Friars

Fray Horra was replaced by Fray Juan Francisco Martín, who joined the mission on December 3, 1797. He was a talented builder and helped the neophytes with their work. He took the time to learn the Salinan language so that he could communicate with the neophytes at the mission.

Cattle were very important at the mission. They provided milk, meat, and leather.

After Fray Martín's arrival, work at Mission San Miguel Arcángel continued, and by the end of the month, three buildings were finished. One was a large building, 71 feet by 17 feet, made of boards. There was also an adobe house, which measured 57 feet by 17 feet. A small adobe chapel, 28 feet by 34 feet, was also built. All three of these buildings had roofs made of sticks and mud, and covered with grass.

At this time, the mission had 130 cows and bulls and 531 sheep.

Most of these had been donated by nearby missions so that ranching could begin at Mission San Miguel Arcángel. Farming had begun also, and wheat, corn, barley, and beans were planted and harvested.

In August 1799, Fray Sitjar left Mission San Miguel Arcángel to return to Mission San Antonio de Padua. Fray Baltasar Carnicier came to Mission San Miguel Arcángel to assist Fray Martín. By December 31, 1800, five more adobe buildings with mud roofs had been built. These included a dormitory for unmarried neophyte women and girls, called a *monjerío*, a granary for storing grain, and a permanent adobe dwelling for the friars, called a *convento*.

A Poisioning

Everything seemed to be going well at Mission San Miguel Arcángel until 1801, when Fray Martín and Fray Carnicier got sick. They developed severe stomach pains and thought that some of the neophytes might have poisoned them. Fray Francisco Pujol came down from Mission San Antonio de Padua to help the two friars, and he became sick as well.

▲
The friars may have wrongly punished the neophytes.

Fray Martín and Fray Carnicier got better, but Fray Pujol died. The friars accused some of the neophytes of poisoning them and had them beaten for the crime. Later, people realized that the neophytes probably had been wrongly accused. Fray Lasuén wrote in his journals that the true cause of the poisonings was a copper container lined with tin that held the friars' liquor. He believed that the container had become toxic and poisoned the drink. Today, some scholars believe that the friars were already sick and that the neophytes tried to heal them by giving them herbal medicines. The friars were not used to these herbal medicines, and the herbs made them sicker.

The Building Continues

By 1804, hundreds of Salinans had converted to Christianity and come to live at the mission. Mission San Miguel Arcángel had all the spinning wheels, looms, and wool it needed for the women to begin weaving blankets and cloth and making clothes. This became one of the principal industries at the mission. The neophytes were successfully raising oxen, cattle, horses, sheep, mules, and pigs. Crops were planted and harvested in greater numbers than ever before.

The above loom is on display at Mission San Miguel Arcángel.

26

The year 1805 was an important year for building. The neophytes constructed 47 houses for the neophyte village, called a *ranchería*, just outside the mission. Mission San Miguel Arcángel had made great progress in just a few years.

A Fire and Its Effects

On August 25, 1806, a devastating fire ripped through Mission San Miguel Arcángel. The blaze destroyed two rows of buildings, the church roof, and more than 6,000 bushels of grain. The friars and the neophytes were discouraged but determined to continue their work. Nearby missions sent food and other materials to help the residents rebuild the damaged buildings.

Restoration began soon after the fire. Many of the buildings were only in need of repairs. Some of the weaving rooms and workshops had to be entirely rebuilt. At the same time, 27 new homes for the neophytes were constructed in the *ranchería*.

Tools like the ones above were used to build the mission.

One of the reasons that the fire had spread so quickly was because the roofs were made of mud, sticks, and thatch. These materials caught fire easily. The friars decided to build tile roofs instead. The friars showed the neophytes how to make tiles from water and clay. The tiles were rounded by molding the wet clay mixture against logs. Then they were left to dry in the sun. The tiles would be much more fire resistant than the roofs that contained sticks and thatch.

Although Mission San Miguel Arcángel had suffered a setback, the Salinans continued to live and work there. At the end of 1806, there were 949 neophytes at the mission and its *ranchería*.

The Finishing Touches

When making the walls, the workers had left holes in the buildings for windows. Glass was difficult to get in Alta California. Instead of covering the windows with glass, neophytes greased and stretched sheepskin over the openings to keep out the cold, rain, and flies. The skin wasn't clear like glass, but it allowed light to enter the buildings.

Once the tile roofs were finished, the neophytes plastered the buildings' walls. To make the plaster, they mixed sand, water, cactus juice, and lime (a powder made from calcium in rocks or seashells). They smoothed the plaster over the rough adobe bricks.

As more buildings were added to the mission, they were placed in the shape of a quadrangle, or hollow square. In the center of the mission quadrangle was a courtyard. As the construction continued, the complex was expanded so that it eventually included the *convento*, *monjerío*, *ranchería*, dining rooms, kitchens, study rooms, workshops, granaries, stables, a corral, and a cemetery.

Ranchos

The lands surrounding the mission were used for planting crops and raising livestock. The mission grew so large that the friars established several *ranchos* for raising livestock. These were built miles from the main mission complex so the friars could work with the American Indians who lived in these areas. The *ranchos* usually had a chapel, stables, a corral, and housing for the neophytes. The *ranchos* at Mission San Miguel Arcángel included Rancho la Playa at San Simeón, Rancho de la Asunción, Rancho del Aguaje, Rancho el Paso de Robles, Rancho Santa Rosa, and Rancho Santa Ysabel.

The first *rancho* was begun in 1810, when a house and granary was built at Rancho la Playa. The rest of the *ranchos* were built between 1810 and 1820. There were hot springs at Rancho el Paso de Robles and Rancho de la Asunción that the friars and neophytes used during the cold, damp winters. The *ranchos* greatly added to Mission San Miguel Arcángel's ability to attract more neophytes and to raise livestock and farm.

Life at Mission San Miguel Arcángel

Change for the Salinans

When the Salinans came to join Mission San Miguel Arcángel, their way of life was greatly changed. The neophytes were treated as children and had to obey the friars. They could not make their own decisions about what they wanted to do or wear. They could not worship the spirits of the Salinan religion. In addition to this lack of basic freedom, the neophytes had to follow a daily routine of work and prayer. The missionaries were used to living lives that followed a strict schedule. The Salinans were not. Many neophytes had trouble adapting to the highly structured lifestyle of the friars, but many felt it was worth it.

The Daily Routine

At dawn, the mission bells woke the neophytes. They gathered for church services, followed by Bible lessons. The women then served a breakfast of *atole*, a mush made of grain or corn. Next, the friars gave everyone his or her work assignment. The men labored in the fields, orchards, *ranchos*, and workshops, while the women tended the children and made food, baskets, cloth, and soap.

The Salinan men grew corn, peas, beans, and barley. They also learned how to make charcoal, which was used for fuel and in paints. On the *ranchos*, they tended to the livestock, which included sheep, cattle, horses, mules, oxen, pigs, and goats. The Salinan men also worked in the mission's workshops to perfect skills in blacksmithing, carpentry, tanning, and making tiles and adobe. When the mission needed repairs, the men worked with the friars to rebuild or refinish the buildings.

Special bells were sometimes used to call the neophytes to Mass. ▶

Chairs like these had seats that were made from hides.

The Salinan women made food for the residents at the mission. They learned Spanish cooking techniques and began to use corn and wheat flour instead of acorn flour. Women were taught to spin yarn out of the wool from sheep raised at the mission. They were taught to weave on looms so they could make blankets and European-style clothing. They made soap by using fat from animals, called tallow, and ashes.

After the morning work session, the women served a lunch of *pozole*, a soup made of grain with a little meat and vegetables. Then it was time for a *siesta*, or rest. Work continued in the afternoon, followed by Mass, supper, and prayers. In the evening, the neophyte boys were taught Spanish and religious lessons. Then everyone had time to relax. The Salinans liked to play games, sing, and dance.

Holidays

Sometimes, everyone at Mission San Miguel Arcángel celebrated church holidays or other occasions with festivals, called *fiestas*. The Spanish holidays were often in honor of Jesus or of Catholic saints. The Salinans liked to celebrate their traditional ceremonies, even if they were not part of their new Catholic faith. While the friars did not approve of these rituals, they didn't stop them. They believed it was more important to keep the neophytes happy. They didn't want the Salinans to get angry and try to leave the mission.

The neophytes sometimes performed their own traditional ceremonies.

Mission San Miguel Arcángel Continues to Grow

A New Church

By 1814, there were 1,076 neophytes at Mission San Miguel Arcángel. This was the greatest number of neophytes that would ever live there. Fray Martín and Fray Cabot, who had come to replace Fray Carnicier, decided that there were so many neophytes at Mission San Miguel Arcángel that a new church was needed. They wrote to ask the governor of California, Governor José Arguello, for a permit to build a larger church.

While the friars were waiting for the governor's response, Fray Cabot decided to set out on an expedition to bring more California Indians to the mission. On October 2, 1814, Fray Cabot and a soldier traveled east to a Yokut Indian village called Bubal. That day, Fray Cabot baptized 22 Yokuts. Twenty of these were over 80 years old. Two others were in their 30s, but were very ill and about to die. It was much easier for the friars to get sick or old people to agree to be baptized than to get healthy adults to convert. The friars believed that only Christians who had been baptized would go to heaven. They told sick or dying people about the terrible things that might happen to them if they didn't go to heaven after they died. When California Indians who were dying heard

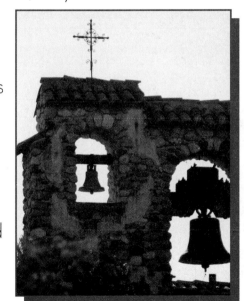

The bell tower.

The friars wanted to baptize as many California Indians as possible.

this, they often agreed to convert.

Fray Cabot left the village of Bubal the next day and traveled to another Yokut village called Sumtache. The Yokuts thought that the Spaniards had come to attack them, and a fight broke out. Two Yokut women and

The neophytes made thousands of adobe bricks for the new church.

two horses were killed. Fray Cabot returned home to Mission San Miguel Arcángel.

On December 14, 1814, Governor Arguello gave Fray Martín and Fray Cabot permission to build a new church. The friars spent over a year planning and gathering the necessary materials. The neophytes made and stored adobe bricks. In 1816, the

Adobe bricks.

stone foundation for the new church was laid. Work continued steadily over the next two years, and in 1818, the new church was finished.

An Attack on the Mission

In 1818, Yokuts from the San Joaquin Valley confronted the Spanish in two battles away from the main complex. The Yokuts may have been angry that the missionaries were taking more and more land in Alta California. The Yokuts who attacked the soldiers found that their bows and arrows were no match for the guns of the Spanish soldiers. They were forced to give up the fight when the soldiers shot back at them with bullets.

Yokuts and the Spanish fought two battles near Mission San Miguel Arcángel in 1818.

Hardships of Mission Life

Hardships for the Spanish

Life at Mission San Miguel Arcángel presented challenges for everyone living there. The buildings had dirt floors, the blankets were coarse and scratchy, and the food was often bland. The missionaries and soldiers were far away from their homes and families, and often felt isolated. The friars had to manage large farms and try to keep hundreds of neophytes happy with their life at the mission.

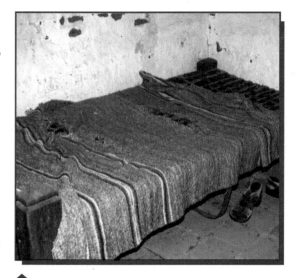

A friar's bed.

Hardships for the Neophytes

Many of the Salinans at Mission San Miguel Arcángel did not like their loss of freedom. Some neophytes had come to the mission only for the food and shelter it provided. They did not like being forced to obey the friars and being punished if they failed to obey. Some neophytes were unhappy with mission life and wanted to leave. To ease the tension at the mission, the friars allowed the Indians to choose *alcaldes*, who were like police officers. They communicated between the friars and the neophytes and tried to keep things peaceful. They also helped to oversee the neophytes' work, and they punished those who were lazy or did not do their jobs well.

Some neophytes tried to escape. The friars sent soldiers and

Life at Mission San Miguel Arcángel was often difficult for both the Spanish and the Salinans.

Neophytes were often punished with whippings.

alcaldes to bring them back. Runaways were beaten. This discouraged others from trying to leave. Another common punishment was locking neophytes in the stocks. Stocks were wooden frames that had holes to hold a prisoner's wrists or ankles and keep him or her confined. At various missions throughout Alta California, the punishments could be very brutal. Word of this treatment spread throughout the mission system and territory, causing fear and anger among some of the Indians.

Illness

Sickness was common at Mission San Miguel Arcángel and caused many deaths. The neophytes were exposed to European diseases for the first time. These diseases included chicken pox, syphilis, measles, and smallpox. While some of these illnesses didn't kill Europeans, they were very harmful to the California Indians, whose bodies had not developed any resistance to them. As a result, many died.

Living quarters were often crowded and sometimes unsanitary. The Salinan women got sick from being inside of the *monjerío* for much of the day and all through the night. Since the buildings were constructed of adobe, the air was damp and cool inside. This caused breathing problems for some people.

The mission system had its advantages and its drawbacks. While it offered the benefits of food and shelter, it also contributed to disease, death, and the loss of freedom for the Salinans.

▲
Hundreds of Salinans died of European diseases at Mission San Miguel Arcángel.

The Decline of Mission San Miguel Arcángel

New Spain Becomes Mexico

In 1821, Mexico gained its independence from Spain after an 11-year war. Alta California and the mission chain became the property of the Mexican government. Ten years later, the Mexican government decided to take control of the mission lands away from the church, an act called secularization. The Spanish had originally planned to secularize all the missions after 10 years, but this had not happened. The friars didn't want the missions to be secularized because they didn't believe that the Indians could operate the missions on their own.

Decoration of the Church

During this period, fewer Salinans were joining Mission San Miguel Arcángel, so new buildings did not need to be built. Fray Martín asked a friend named Estévan Munras to come help the neophytes paint pictures on the walls inside the church. Munras is responsible for the bright and colorful frescoes inside the mission church.

The artists at Mission San Miguel Arcángel had to make their own paints. To do this, they added linseed oil or cactus juice to dyes and pigments. Most dyes were made from materials that could be found in the area. Yellow was created with a clay called ochre. Mercury ore made red, and copper ore made green. Black came from charcoal.

▲ *Pigments like these were used to make paint.*

42

Mission San Miguel Arcángel's altar wall is covered with religious symbols and designs. ▶

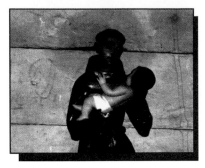

▲ *Statue of Saint Anthony.*

Munras wanted to paint designs that would make the inside of the church of Mission San Miguel Arcángel look like ancient Roman buildings. Since the mission didn't have the materials to build detailed doorways, arches, balconies, and pillars, Munras and the neophytes painted them instead. The artists used a technique called marbleizing, which made objects look like they were carved from marble.

These paintings create the illusion that the arches and pillars are actually there.

In front of the church sanctuary is an altar. Behind the altar is the reredos (a large backboard) that has an eye painted on it. This represents the all-seeing eye of God. Below are three statues. A statue of the mission's namesake, Saint Michael, is in the center. Statues of Saint Anthony, the patron saint of the poor, and Saint Francis of Assisi, the founder of

▲ *Statue of Saint Francis of Assisi.*

the Franciscan order, are on either side. The friars used these objects when teaching the neophytes religious lessons. They used the statues and pictures to illustrate their stories.

Secularization

Fray Martín died at the mission in 1824. Fray Cabot, took charge of Mission San Miguel Arcángel. Soon after, major changes began to take place. In 1826, the Mexican government passed laws to emancipate, or free, the neophytes at the missions. Although the government said that the neophytes were free from the rule of the friars, it made it legal for the Mexican officials to force the California Indians to work the land that was taken from the Catholic church. On January 6, 1831, the Mexican governor of California, Governor Echeandia issued a decree saying that the missions would be secularized. That day, four Mexican officials came to Mission San Miguel Arcángel to free the neophytes from the friars. One of the officials, José Castro, assembled the Salinans at the mission and told them that they were emancipated. The Salinans asked to consider the offer overnight. The

▲

Juan Bautista Alvarado talking to the neophytes.

next morning, most of the neophytes declined the offer. They said that they were poor and would be better off at the mission.

Another official, Juan Bautista Alvarado, thought that the neophytes didn't understand the benefits of emancipation, so he jumped on a *carreta*, or cart, to address the crowd. After he discussed emancipation, he told those who wanted to leave to stand to the right. Anyone wishing to stay was to stand to the left. Most of

Many Indians became vaqueros.

the neophytes went to the left, showing that they wanted to stay. The Salinans said: "We want to remain with the padre [the friar]. He is very good to us and we like him."

On August 9, 1834, the Mexican government seized the mission. The friars were allowed to stay and conduct church activities, but they could no longer make the neophytes work or tell them what to do. The government appointed Mexican officials to run the mission. The first official was Ignácio Coronél, who arrived on July 14, 1836. Coronél didn't stay long and was replaced by Ynocente García. Both men were harsh with the Salinans, so many left the mission. Some found jobs as cowboys called *vaqueros* or as servants on ranches in the area. Others tried to return to their old villages, but ranchers and settlers had taken their lands, and the old villages no longer existed. Many Salinans had grown up at the mission and didn't know how to live off the land like their ancestors had in the past.

Hunger

As more and more neophytes left the mission, fewer crops were produced. Food became scarce, and starvation gripped Mission San Miguel Arcángel in the late 1830s and early 1840s. Fray Ramón Abella came to Mission San Miguel Arcángel in December 1840. The mission faced severe food shortages, and Fray Abella had to leave in 1841. He went to Mission San Luis Obispo, where, even though he was close to starvation, he shared his food with the hungry neophytes.

The Mission Is Sold

Under secularization, many mission lands that were supposed to be returned to the California Indians were sold or given away by Mexican officials. Two businessmen, Petronillo Ríos and William Reed, bought Mission San Miguel Arcángel in 1846. Then, in 1848, gold was discovered in Coloma, California, and eager miners began to flood into Alta California. Many Americans moved into the territory, and soon war broke out between the United States and Mexico. The Americans won the war and took possession of Alta California. It became the 31st state in 1850, and its name was shortened to California.

▲

Americans moved to Alta California to find gold.

The Americans who took over California also treated the Salinans and other Indians poorly. Like the Spanish, they viewed the Indians as being inferior to themselves. Many of the new American settlers forced the Salinans off of their lands. Today, few people of Salinan descent remain. Most of the Salinans either died or joined the American people and the American culture.

The Mission Today

The Mission Is Returned to the Church

Mission San Miguel Arcángel continued to decay. In 1859, the complex was returned to the Catholics by U.S. President James Buchanan. However, it wasn't until 1878 that the Reverend Philip Farrelly was sent to start up a parish church once again. In the meantime, some of the mission buildings were rented out. They were used to house a saloon, a sewing machine store, a dance hall, and living quarters.

President Buchanan.

The town of San Miguel began to thrive after 1886, when railroad tracks were laid down near the town, connecting it to Paso Robles and other towns in California. Many Chinese laborers helped build the railroad tracks. Now people could travel easily to and from San Miguel, which increased business in the area. In 1897, the town celebrated its early history by hosting a centennial of the mission's founding. Parades, dancing, lectures, and concerts were included in the celebration.

Many people wanted to restore Mission San Miguel Arcángel, which was crumbling out of neglect. In 1928, the mission was returned to the care of the Franciscan order. The friars began major repairs. Today, Franciscans live at the restored mission, which also serves as a parish church, retreat center, and museum. The mission hosts a *fiesta* on the third Sunday of September each year. At the *fiesta*, visitors can learn more about the mission's history.

◀ *Friars still live and work at Mission San Miguel Arcángel.*

▲ *Neophytes cooked in ovens like this one at Mission San Miguel Arcángel.*

Many students visit the mission's museum to see how the friars and Salinan Indians lived years ago. Visitors can walk through an old kitchen and see a brick oven that the neophytes used for baking. They can visit the friars' living quarters, view their rustic beds and other furniture, and see windows that are still covered with sheepskin. Tools, a loom, a wine vat, and pigments like those used by the Salinans are also on display. Baskets made by California Indians, artifacts from the railroad's Chinese workers, and vestments worn by the friars are included in the museum. Evidence of earthquakes is still visible in the church. Cracks in the plaster run along the walls from the roof to the floor. Although the church's artwork has survived remarkably well, some of it shows signs of water stains and cracks.

The influence of the Spanish missions is still evident in California today. Farming and ranching, two skills brought to the area

▲ *Cracks can be seen in the plaster walls.*

by the Spanish more than 200 years ago, thrive in California. The state is now a world leader in agricultural production.

Artifacts and literature about the Salinan people are displayed in the Salinan Nation Adobe Cultural Center. Each year, Salinan descendants gather at Mission San Antonio de Padua in Jolon, California, to celebrate their heritage.

▲ *Artifacts are on display inside the mission.*

Today, Mission San Miguel Arcángel stands as a monument to the early Californians. It helps visitors understand what life was like during the late 1700s and early 1800s. The mission complex teaches present-day Americans about the lives of the Salinans and the Catholic friars who helped to make California the success it is today.

▲ *The mission today.*

Build Your Own
Mission San Miguel Arcángel

To make your own model of the San Miguel Arcángel mission, you will need:

Styrofoam
pencil
glue
corrugated cardboard
X-Acto knife (ask an adult for help)
moss

brown paint
colored paper
miniature bell
scissors
ruler
foamcore (16" x 16")

Directions

Step 1: To make the front and back of the church, cut out two pieces of Styrofoam that are 12" by 9".

Adult supervision is suggested.

Step 2: Choose one of the pieces to be the front and cut out a door with an X-Acto knife.

Step 3: Cut two pieces of Styrofoam that are 12″ by 9″. These will be the sides of the church.

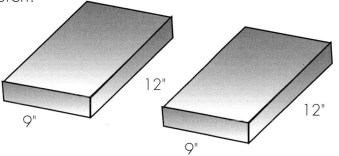

Step 4: Arrange all four pieces in a box shape and glue together. Hold in place for 30 seconds or until the glue dries.

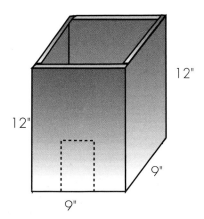

Step 5: Use the large piece of foamcore for the base. Attach the church building to the base with glue.

Step 6: Cut out two Styrofoam triangles whose bases are 9" long and whose sides are each 6". Glue to the top of the front and back church walls.

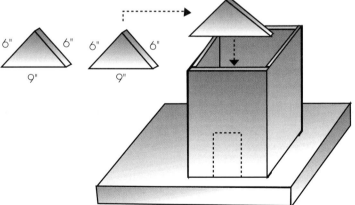

Step 7: To make the arcade, cut two pieces of Styrofoam that are 3" by 7". These are the front and back pieces.

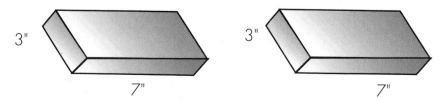

Step 8: Trace two arched doorways in the middle of each Styrofoam arcade wall and cut them out with an X-Acto knife.

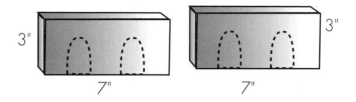

Step 9: To make the arcade roof, cut out a piece of cardboard that is 5" by 8". Paint the cardboard roof brown. Let paint dry.

Step 10: Glue the two arcade pieces to the back left side of the church. Then glue the roof to the arcade.

Step 11: To make windows on the church, cut out small squares of cardboard and glue them on the building.

Step 12: Time to decorate! Cut out colored paper in tiny squares and glue to the floor of the church. Use a round piece of blue paper for an indoor fountain.

overview

fountain

paper squares

Step 13: Glue a miniature bell in the doorway of the church. Cut paper to make a cross and glue on the front of the church.

Step 14: Place glue around your mission and arrange moss, dried flowers, or fake plants.

*Use the above mission as a reference for building your mission.

Important Dates in Mission History

1492	Christopher Columbus reaches the West Indies
1542	Cabrillo's expedition to California
1602	Sebastián Vizcaíno sails to California
1713	Fray Junípero Serra is born
1769	Founding of San Diego de Alcalá
1770	Founding of San Carlos Borromeo del Río Carmelo
1771	Founding of San Antonio de Padua and San Gabriel Arcángel
1772	Founding of San Luis Obispo de Tolosa
1775–76	Founding of San Juan Capistrano
1776	Founding of San Francisco de Asís
1776	Declaration of Independence is signed
1777	Founding of Santa Clara de Asís
1782	Founding of San Buenaventura
1784	Fray Serra dies
1786	Founding of Santa Bárbara
1787	Founding of La Purísima Concepción
1791	Founding of Santa Cruz and Nuestra Señora de la Soledad
1797	**Founding of** San José, San Juan Bautista, **San Miguel Arcángel**, and San Fernando Rey de España
1798	Founding of San Luis Rey de Francia
1804	Founding of Santa Inés
1817	Founding of San Rafael Arcángel
1823	Founding of San Francisco de Solano
1849	Gold found in northern California
1850	California becomes the 31st state

Glossary

adobe (uh-DOH-bee) Sun-dried bricks made of straw, mud, and sometimes manure.

baptism (BAP-tih-zum) A ceremony performed when someone is accepted into, or accepts, the Christian faith.

Catholicism (kuh-THAH-lih-sih-zum) The faith or practice of Catholic Christianity, which includes following the spiritual leadership of priests headed by the pope.

Christianity (kris-chee-A-nih-tee) A religion based on the teachings of Jesus Christ and the Bible, practiced by Eastern, Roman Catholic, and Protestant groups.

complex (KAHM-pleks) A large group of buildings.

convert (kun-VIRT) To change from belief in one religion to belief in another religion.

decree (dih-KREE) An official law or order.

emancipation (ih-man-sih-PAY-shun) Freedom.

Franciscan (fran-SIS-kin) A communal Roman Catholic order of friars, or "brothers," who follow the teachings and example of Saint Francis of Assisi, who did much work as a missionary.

fresco (FRES-koh) A painting made on wet plaster, which lasts longer than a painting made on a dry wall.

friar (FRY-ur) A brother in a communal religious order. Friars can also be priests

granary (GRAY-nuh-ree) A building where grain is stored.

livestock (LYV-stahk) Farm animals kept for use or profit.

Mass (MAS) A Christian religious ceremony.

neophyte (NEE-uh-fyt) Name for an American Indian once he or she was baptized into the Christian religion.

quarters (KWOR-turz) Rooms where someone lives.

ranching (RAN-ching) Raising cattle, horses, or sheep on a farm.

restoration (res-tuh-RAY-shun) Working to return something, like a building, to its original state.

sanctuary (SAYNK-choo-weh-ree) The sacred part of a church, which contains the altar.

secularization (seh-kyuh-luh-rih-ZAY-shun) When the operation of the mission lands was turned over to the Christian Indians.

thatch (THACH) A covering for a house made up of reeds and grass bundled together.

vestments (VEST-mints) Robes that are worn for special ceremonies.

viceroy (VYS-roy) A governor who rules and acts as the representative of the king.

Pronunciation Guide

alcaldes (ahl-KAHL-dez)

atole (ah-TOL-ay)

carretas (kah-REH-tahs)

convento (kahn-VEN-toh)

fiestas (fee-EHS-tahs)

fray (FRAY)

monjerío (mohn-HAYR-ee-oh)

padre (PAH-dray)

pozole (poh-ZOH-lay)

rancherías (RAHN-cher-EE-as)

ranchos (RAHN-chohs)

siesta (see-EHS-tah)

vaqueros (bah-KEHR-ohs)

Resources

For more information on the California missions, check out these books and Web sites:

Books:

Bleeker, Sonia. *The Mission Indians of California.* New York, NY: William Morrow and Company, 1956.

Iverson, Eva C. *California's Mission San Miguel Arcángel.* San Miguel, CA: Franciscan Padres, no date.

Oh California. Boston, MA: Houghton Mifflin Co., 1991.

Robinson, Alfred. *Life in California.* Santa Barbara, CA: Peregrin Smith, Inc., 1970.

Web Sites:

California Missions Resource Page
   http://www.csd.k12.ca.us/coyote_canyon/4/missions/mission_ndx.html

Spanish Missions of California
   http://tqd.advanced.org/3615/

Index